ABOUT THE AUTHOR

Valerie Gascoyne was born in Wimbledon.

She has always been creatively driven and began writing poetry when she was a teenager. Valerie got involved in writing lyrics for songs and in the early '80s wrote the lyrics to 'Come Another Day' which was released in Norway through M.A.M. music. She continued to write poetry and has had some individual poems printed in various anthologies. She is passionate about words and all forms of creative expression, including Art and Music.

This is Valerie's first collection to be published. Some of the poems are inspired by her own personal experiences, others are observational.

VALERIE GASCOYNE

Angels and Elephants

AUSTIN MACAULEY PUBLISHERS™
LONDON • CAMBRIDGE • NEW YORK • SHARJAH

A CIP catalogue record for this title is available from the British Library.

ISBN 9781398412347 (Paperback)
ISBN 9781398412354 (ePub e-book)

www.austinmacauley.com

First Published (2021)
Austin Macauley Publishers Ltd
25 Canada Square
Canary Wharf
London
E14 5LQ

DEDICATION

For Aimée and Charlie

ACKNOWLEDGEMENTS

With love and appreciation to my supportive husband Tony.

Special thanks to the talented illustrator Anna Twarog for her sensitive visual interpretation of my poetry.

POEMS

This Too Will Pass

So, the world has fallen apart
The NHS have stolen our hearts
We are clapping for them, lighting candles
Ringing bells
While they are standing at the gates of hell
Just when we thought all hope had gone
Captain Tom kept walking on
Now we stay home and remember when
We had our freedom and could see our friends
It does not seem that long ago
When we were free to get up and go
Now we live in fear, we live in fright
Praying to get through another night
Waking up to another bad news day
As Covid-19 has its evil way
Restrictions have been put into place
Those that defy are in disgrace
This life, this time is so surreal
Sadly, it is all too real
When we get through this
We will count our blessings
Missing those that are gone
All too distressing
Never will we forget this unprecedented time
Or take for granted any other day
When children could go out to play
We could socialise without a care
Before the madness and despair
Things that seemed so important
They are just things
What we are missing most of all
Are the simple pleasures
Family and friends
The only true joy that this life brings.

JOY HEROES
FAMILY PRAYING
WE WILL REMEMBER
BLESSINGS
CHILDREN
FRIENDS
N
H
S

These Times

In between times of feeling grateful
Sometimes I sit and cry
For the freedom that we have recently lost
While we are living to die
We are dying to live
But we cannot
With restrictions on our lives
The future looks bleak,
Controlled by those who think they know best
They may be right they may be wrong
I just feel so depressed
No more birthday celebrations
Or weddings to attend
No Wimbledon or Queens
Holidays on airplanes
Are only in our dreams
I am trying to be positive
To see the good in things
Some days this really works
Most of the time, I just feel anxious
Like there is some underlying plan
Some mystery that I cannot see
That is destroying all humanity
I hope I am wrong, must stay
  strong
Until this time moves on.

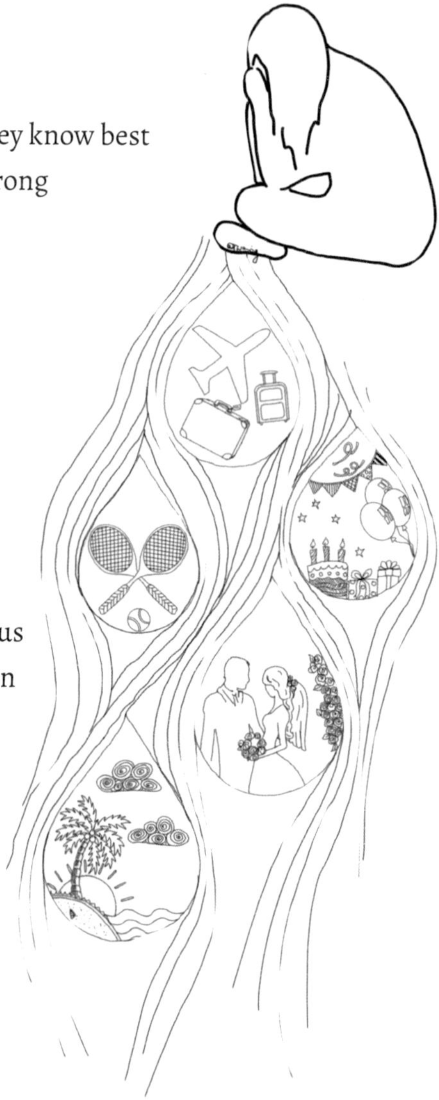

The Big Pause

We must remember what this time has taught us
In between feeling anxious and afraid
Maybe we had become too greedy
In pursuit of the next best thing
We were the have it all brigade
Storing things up we did not need
While pursuing something new
Chasing papier-mâché dreams
Which were never going to come true
What were we thinking, with our frantic lives
Never having time for anyone
With our busy schedule filled with work and fun
It took a pandemic to make us stop
To look within ourselves and not without
To make us realise what matters most
It is like we knew but didn't know
Just a glimpse of appreciating the now
Not the future or the past
Just this time which will not last
We learned that we could live without
Foreign holidays, theatres, and concerts,
Flying here and there on airplanes
So much has changed to change our minds
Being locked down has made us kind
Appreciating so much more
The true things that are worth living for
Family, friends that we hold dear
More precious than anything,
Cherish them, love them and keep
  them near.

Covid Winter 2020

The days grew shorter and the children cried
They were so afraid of the dark
The earth trembled with terror
The trees shook with fear
Still the pandemic raged on
The people were more than afraid than ever
They thought this madness would pass
Then the months rolled by
The economy destroyed
Working from home
Meant more unemployed
No plans could be made
Without disarray
Families torn apart as never before
Through no fault of their own
Some people were left alone and lonely
The government tried their best to no avail
Scientists were on their trail
Confusion reigned as never before
The poor were getting poorer
The rich remained the same

Neither one could win, both could only lose
There seemed no solution, a beginning without an end
The planet tossed into turmoil
Spinning and spinning, hoping to mend
With a vaccine bringing springs of hope
To allay our fears and help us cope
Some are relieved, others are afraid
Thinking there is a choice.

Painted Sky

God is painting the sky again
The angels are helping too
They must have so much fun
Deciding what to do
Pink, blue, red, and yellow
They move around without a sound
A kaleidoscope of colours
In an ever-changing hue
Every day is different
I must keep looking before they fade
So vivid and clear before erased
God is painting the sky so beautiful
Be quick, don't do anything else
Just treasure this sunset
While it lasts.

The Elephant in the Room

The elephant sat in the room: 'My name is grief,' she said
'I will not be leaving any time soon, for the one you love is dead.'
'But things will surely get better in time,' I asked so pleadingly
'Not at all, they never will,' is what she said to me

For time it flies when someone dies but also it stands still
All the memories are stored, never to be replaced
You will never hear their voice again or see their smiling face
Your friends they try to understand and hope that you will see

That time's the greatest healer, time will set you free
They do not want to talk about the elephant in the room
That is full of gloom, they feel you should move on
The fear, the fright it scares them so, in case it touches them

So, you try to hide the grief you feel
It does not always work, you are sometimes caught off-guard
A song, a smell, a breeze, the sky, it has never been so hard
It is the worst thing that you have ever felt
There is no peace or calm and no release

'Am I going quite insane?' you ask the elephant in the room
'Not at all, my dear one, the pain you feel is true
It is something you will have to live with
While life goes on and grows around you

It will never leave, you will always grieve
So much it will astound you.'
'What advice may you give to help me through,' I say
The elephant looked me in the eye and said
'Just take it day by day.'

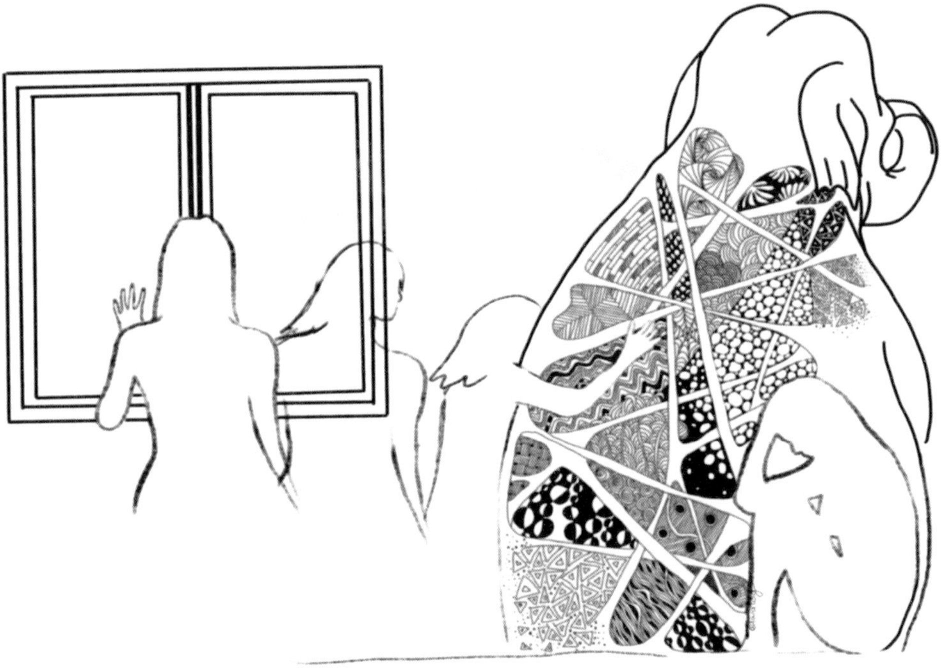

Angels

I saw an Angel in the sky
I often see them passing by
They are watching over us on earth
Have been doing so before our birth
They hear our thoughts and see our deeds
Both good and bad and those in between
They watch us as we bend and break
Worrying about tomorrow
The love we give the love we take
Our happiness and sorrow
They see us create our karma
Living our own drama
While we drift through life so unaware
The days go by so fast like a river
With the blink of an eye, they are gone
Like the Angel in the sky.

Angels Watching

Humans with their busy lives
We are watching over you
Angels guiding you gently
Just believe that we are true
You are given free will
To choose your own way
We sometimes sit and cry for you
Forever and a day
Free will it is good and bad
For sometimes it just makes you sad
When you take the wrong turn again
You feel so much human pain
If you would only speak to us more
We could help you beyond belief
You are blessed more than you know.

When the Sun Comes Out

It is very easy when the sun comes out to believe that it's going to shine forever
And it's very easy when you're with me to believe that we will always be together
Then the clouds appear, the rain comes down, and that is how I feel every time you leave me
It seems so unfair that I cannot share my life with you completely
So, I will keep you here until you disappear
Then I will do my best to get along without you
I will hope in my heart when we are apart
That someday, some way you will miss me too
If it is not to be that you will be with me
Then my love I must accept it
And I will keep your smile inside my heart
But you will never know I kept it.

Lady Sunshine,
for Diana Princess of Wales

Lady Sunshine what has happened to you
You came here with so much to do
Lady Sunshine you were so unaware
Of the evil which lay everywhere
You had a touch of innocence about you
That the tougher kind just took in their stride
As I sit here writing about you
I cannot understand why you have died
For I see so many around taking all they can
They never think of giving a thing
I think you learned a long time ago
Something they may never know
Simply the joy that giving can bring
Lady Sunshine you looked so well
With your beauty and insecurity
There were times that you stumbled and fell
I know it wasn't easy to know life isn't easy
Princess of our time
Your beauty will live on Lady Sunshine.

The Wind

I am the wind
My friend is the air
We are both invisible
But everywhere
We can change our state
Change our mind
We can change your view
Moving clouds and trees
If we choose to
Sometimes blowing calming
Sometimes dancing wildly
Always omnipresent
Always there.

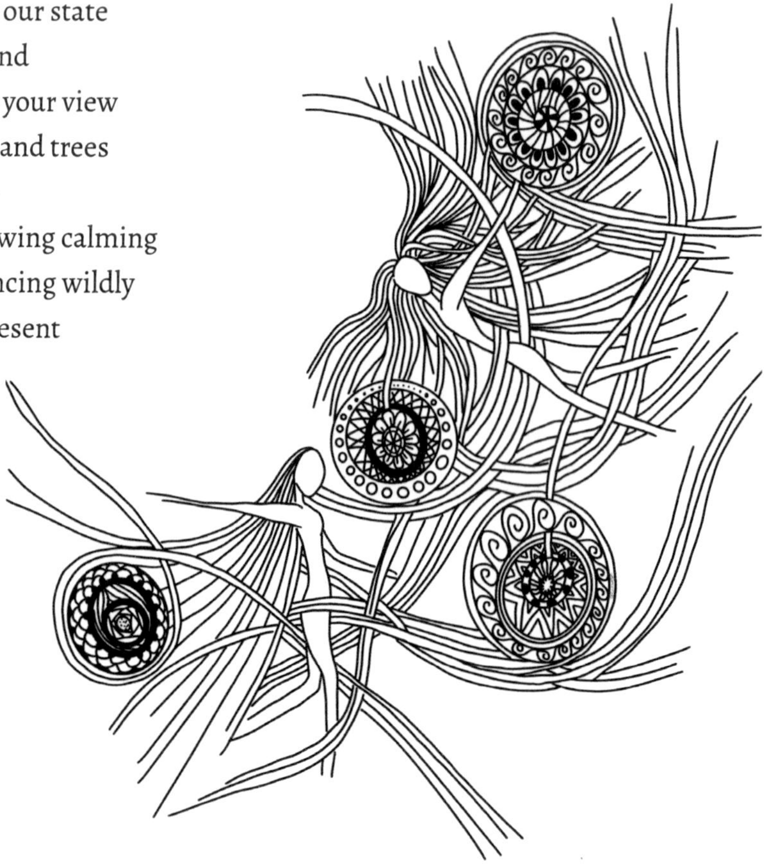

Photograph

I came across a photograph of you
Smiling and happy
To be fair it was taken some time ago
I have not seen that smile for a long time
What happened to you and me
We had it all then set it free
Thought something better was waiting
Something better than you and me
So, we made a choice to let us go
Took our separate paths
We meet sometimes in awkward moments
Children bind us together forever
Our love for them is boundless
It is not their fault the path we chose
We are still their family
Broken but not smashed
The love we shared is in their eyes
We make things work in different ways
Friends but on another level
I think it is called uncoupling these days
It could be worse it could be better
We are where we are with a life to live
It is so important to forgive
Enjoy our days those that remain
And let me see you smile again.

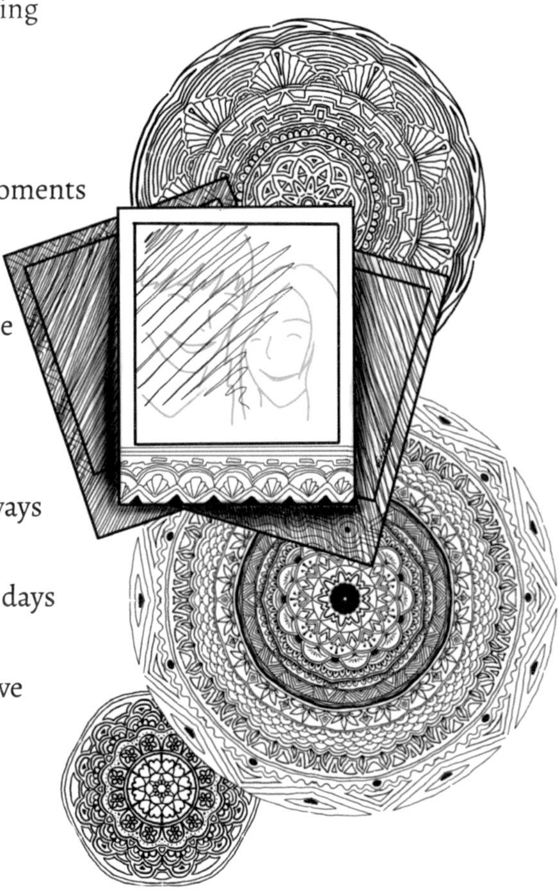

Ripples

We are all just pebbles on the beach
We make ripples in our lives
That have so much reach
Every ripple affects another
Be they family, friend or lover
The ripples flow forward forever and a day
Long after we have gone
The ripples flow on and on
They leave memories of love and hope
For those who cannot cope
On and on they go
With their memories in tow.

Broken Heart

My heart is breaking
Seeing you this way
I never thought this would happen
Never see the day
When the life was ebbing out of you
And there is nothing I can do
Feel so inept so unsure
Cannot deal with this
There is no cure
Would love to make you better
Make you all complete
It is so unfair you are good not bad
But you are in a bad way
Do not want to pass you to strangers
Who do not really care
Praying there is some goodness there
I will be here watching over you
That is the very least that I can do,
Until your time on earth is gone
The best of me had the best of you
We grew up together became careless along the way
Nothing is forever not you not me
Some of us leave early.

Feathers

Angels are remarkably close to me
Watching very carefully
I can sense them and see them in the sky
Floating by
The signs that appear take me by surprise
White feathers float down before my eyes
Comforting to know we are not alone
I speak to them much more these days
Asking them to guide my way
Through this temporary life
On the planet earth
I lived with them before my birth
My guardian angel helped choose my life
To learn lessons and improve my soul
But sometimes I forget.

Irish Blue

I keep thinking I might see you just as you were before your demise
Keep feeling your shadow watching over me like I watched over you
It is so unkind this vacant space
With no one here to take your place
This life with death so hard to understand
Gone too soon and so unplanned
I know you didn't want to go and leave your family
I know you didn't want to stay and be a burden in any way
So off you went and left us here
Without yourself which we hold dear
Before you left, I looked at you
Into your eyes which were Irish blue
I felt the love which we once had
It filled the room, and I was glad
Though nothing would ever be the same
The essence of you remains
I blame myself for not saving you
But I did not know how to.

Winds of Change

I thought the wind had dropped until it lifted me high into the air
Tumbling me around, as I tried to catch my breath
I saw the clouds racing on, I saw your face then it was gone
Looking back and not forwards is not good for anyone
I could smell Autumn in the air at the time you decided to leave
Saw your eyes smiling in adversity
Thrashing about in the confusion of life
I felt searing pain with the whiplash wind
Despair, rain, darkness, pain
Nothing can save you, I can only watch
The leaves trembling with their tears
Sunshine trying to shine through the clouds
Then with a gust of wind you were gone
As I tumbled to the ground.

Grief

Grief stays inside you which you try to hide
Your life grows around you with a heaviness inside
You cannot see a future only the past.
Somehow you know that nothing is going to last
This temporary life with all its ups and downs
Searching for answers, there are none to be found
Why did this happen, life seems so unfair
You see people laughing and try to remember joy
Carefree happier times seem so far away
Tears flow too easily these days
Only memories are left when someone is dead
Running around inside your head
One looks for understanding and feels so out of control
But you know there must be a meaning deep down in your soul.

Life

We do not know why we are here
There are so many questions unanswered
We live our lives mostly in fear
That a new day brings a new task
There are life's lessons to learn at every turn
We are all going to die one day
We do not know where or when
Then we might have to begin again
While we are here, we search for love
For when the world looks grey
Love brightens up our day.

Lonely

Cannot bear to see you lonely it makes me feel so sad,
It is like looking at a life that you never had
But I know you had a lovely life because I shared some time with you,
There were years that were happy,
So fast they flew and birthdays too.
There was a fabric of colour, children, and love
We went our separate ways, and the years flew swiftly by
Tough times, difficulties, all part of life's merry-go-round.
We must remember the good and thank the Lord above,
For now, we sit in silence, in our own separate space
History is our only connection, which cannot be replaced.

Uncle Pat

I met a lonely man today; he had such lot to say,
He talked and talked about his life and how things were without his wife,
He talked about the jobs he had, most were good, none were bad.
He talked about how strong he had been, and how he also met the Queen,
I hoped somehow that even he might wish to hear something of me,
But on he went without a pause; he was a man without a cause
The more he talked it became so clear his was the only voice he wished
  to hear
My patience it was at its best. It was certainly put to the test
The stories he told were quite absurd, still I hung on to every word
The more he talked, I felt so sad, it was about a life he never had.

Teenage Crime

I have no hope I have no fear
My parents they do not seem to care
If they love me, I cannot feel it
If I want something, I steal it
The police catch me
Social workers help me
They blame it on my family
To me it's just a way of life
I carry with me the sharpest knife
To frighten those who don't do as I say
I may even use it again one day
Robbery comes easily
I went to reform school for a while
When they sentenced me, I had to smile
The judge has no idea about my life
With his fancy car and fancy wife
Will I ever change, why should I
I will change the world before I die.

My Children

You can count on me when things go wrong
For you, my dear, I will be strong
The love I feel you will never know
Not until you have a child of your own
No one can deny the pleasure and pain
That comes with a child being born
You are my life ever since we met
From your first cry which I will never forget
Our journey together had begun
So much has happened since way back then
Good times and bad happy and sad
We have been together through the best and the worst
Rising and falling please understand
Don't ever let go of my hand
I am always here never far away
Forever and a day.

How

In this world of good and bad, right and wrong
How can I help you to be strong
When temptation comes knocking at your door
And I am not there to protect you any more
What advice can I give you
That will stand the test of time
For this world that is ever changing
Dear children of mine
What can I say to send you on the right path
To fight with the angels and live in the light
Where truth is truth and right is might
All I can do is love you and hope that some day
You will know just how much I love you
And it will guide you on your way.

Parenthood

We are terrified every day
That some madman will steal our children away
We do not let them walk alone or talk to strangers
We try to warn them of the dangers
That are everywhere
Because of our fears we are overprotective
We make sure their pastimes are extremely selective
Make a fuss if they catch a bus
We drive them everywhere
By appointment only friends come for tea
Play video games and watch TV
With their mobile phones and technology
This is life as they know it
They have everything they need
Except their freedom.

The Song

There is a song that you sing to me
You are probably unaware
That the song that you bring to me
Takes me off somewhere
Sometimes the words don't rhyme
And the melody is off key
Still it makes me feel just fine
The song you sing to me
For this song comes from your heart
Wherever that may be
Far or near I will hold it dear
And I will keep it just for me!

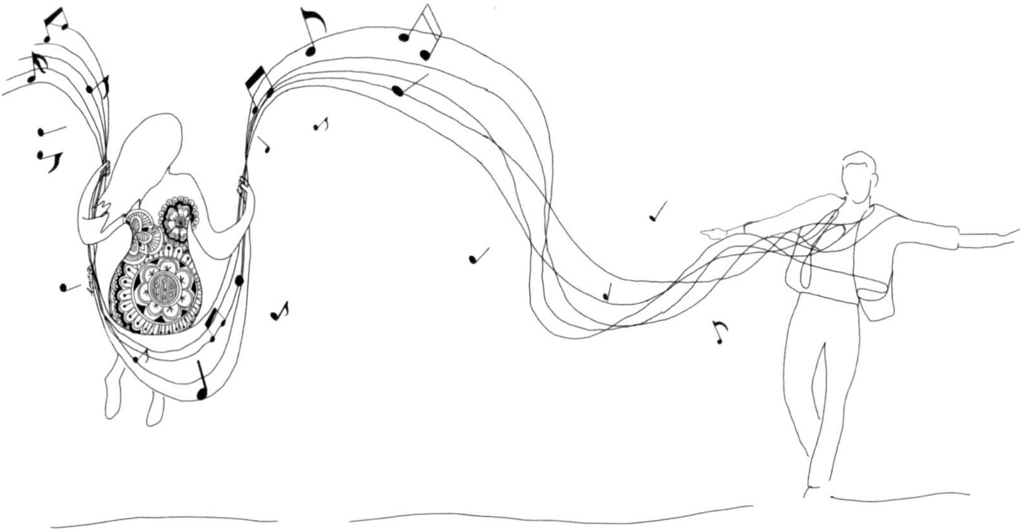

Money

The world revolves around money it is true
If only there was more love shining through
People marry for money under the guise of love
They give no thought to heaven above
Possessions become everything
Love becomes the second string
Men cheat for money, kill for money
Pretend to be your friend
It all comes down to money in the end
Wars are fought over religion it is true
Still someone somewhere is making a buck or two
Out of guns and weapons and violence
All paid for at our expense
Where does the future lie for this imperfect race?
We are destroying our planet it's a downright disgrace
I am talking about you and me
I am sure you will agree
With more love in our hearts
We can make a new start
All over again.

For our children's children
We owe it to them.

Crossing the Line

In the midst of a personal holocaust
I gave myself to you
Thinking you were my friend
Pure good and true
I had much to lose nothing to gain
For your eyes were full of pain
From a broken long-ago dream
I felt obliged to see this through
To feel what crossing the line would do
From friends to lovers
What would we discover
Maybe some comfort we would find
In each other's arms, I was so blind
You ran from me emotionally
I was confused and could not see
What I had done to make you run
A shadow fell across my smile
As you drifted away mile by mile
Our friendship, once an easy chair
Has since become a cross to bear.

Fear of Change

I was so scared I could not see
Through all my pain and misery
My whole small world turned upside down
My home destroyed my hopes all drowned
It took a while to re-adjust
To find my balance
And to trust the universe
To help me through
The pain of living without you
My confidence an all-time low
My carefree stance where did it go
Feeling drained by all that's come and gone
On life's journey that we all must run.

Helpless

In an unguarded moment you smiled at me
You took me by surprise
I saw a look I had never seen before
In your beautiful blue eyes
Strange, I had never noticed them before
Now I want to see them more
My emotions are in turmoil,
My heart is beating fast
Every time I see you
I think will be the last
Why this should concern me
I have no idea
I just seem to need you extremely near
Now I am falling off a mountain top
No safety net in sight
Fighting this battle with all my might
It is a losing battle, I feel lost without a cause
You don't fit into my future
I don't fit into yours
Still here I stand so helpless
My world turned upside down
Feeling so crazy whenever you are around
I should run away screaming
Maybe I am dreaming
But I know that it is true
Please catch me for I am falling
In love with you.

Before You Go

Before you go, search your heart
Remember the love that we once knew
We have shared laughter, tears, and sorrow
In my heart I have always loved you
Count the memories that you have stored there
Will you forget them so fast
All the years we spent together
That sped away so fast
Think of all the grey skies
We turned from grey to blue
Think what my life will be like
If I did not have you
When you walk through this life and you're lonely
Remember I am here and so
The door will always be open
Just thought I would tell you
Before you go.

Love's Dance

While you are lying with another
I think of you and how you are
You came so close in my dream last night
But now you seem so far
If moments could be frozen
Like a pause on a video frame
The time I would have chosen
Is the day you called my name
I have not seen your gentle face
For such a long time
Do you ever think of me
When you were all mine
The years go rushing by
While we are looking the other way
The people we love dance on
To a time so far away
Overall, it's just too bad
That those we love and know
Cannot stay around forever
We have to let them go.

Time and Death

We are all going to die one day
Why is it such a shock
The one thing guaranteed is death
We lose all that we love,
Family, friends, and pets
Grief is the price we pay for love
When love is all there is
Humanity is somewhat flawed
We ask the questions why
What is this life all about
Why do we have to die
Where do we go from here
More questions than answers
For something that we fear.

My Heart

My heart goes out to you
There is nothing I can do
We were over long ago
So why does this concern me so
To see you struggle on alone
No one there when you come home
It was not meant to be this way
We did not know when we parted
Which paths our lives would take
I think at first you were relieved
To have your freedom
It was I who grieved
Now things have changed
I have healed and found some peace
With someone else
Still I worry about you
I wish it wasn't so
I have moved on and let you go
Joy is the wish I have for you
With a companion by your side
It's not easy this life
We all need a friend a steady hand
When all around is not so grand
I would like to take you by the hand
To talk to you about the past
Which is done and dusted and didn't last
We didn't make it but we are still here
Enjoy your life
God bless you dear.

Birdsong

The most beautiful sound that you will ever hear
Is the birds in the morning singing loud and clear
It lifts your soul, it warms your heart
Such a good way to start the day
A gift from Mother Nature
With no strings attached
Singing all the time
The sweetest song
Morning and evening
Sometimes all day long
Where would we be
Without their sweet melody
That they sing to us for free?
Joy perfect joy.

Curtains

Do not grieve for me when I go,
There is a time for everything I know,
Just remember all those times,
We sat so close with two like-minds
But time is like an eagle flying through the sky
It waits for no one not you or I
We must treasure every pleasure while we can
For I am just a woman you a man
God's great plan I do not know
We fit in somewhere like a beautiful rainbow
I will love you every day in every way
Until I am gone like the end of a day.

Hope

When all the world seems dark and crazy
And love seems far away
You cannot see the wood for the trees
Just another hard work day
When the chips are down
Someone has let you down
You do not know where to look or who to trust
Feeling anxious and insecure
This life feels so unsure
When once on steady ground
A smile in the morning, a cup of tea
Can brighten up your day
The sun creeping through the edges of a blind
A bird chirping while in flight
Hope springs eternal in your heart
And you know you will be alright.

Going Home

Lord when you take me
Make me whole
Take my life my dreams
My failures too
My sins good deeds
And all in between
Show me the love
That I know exists
In the universe
Where there are no twists
Everything is perfect
All is perfect love

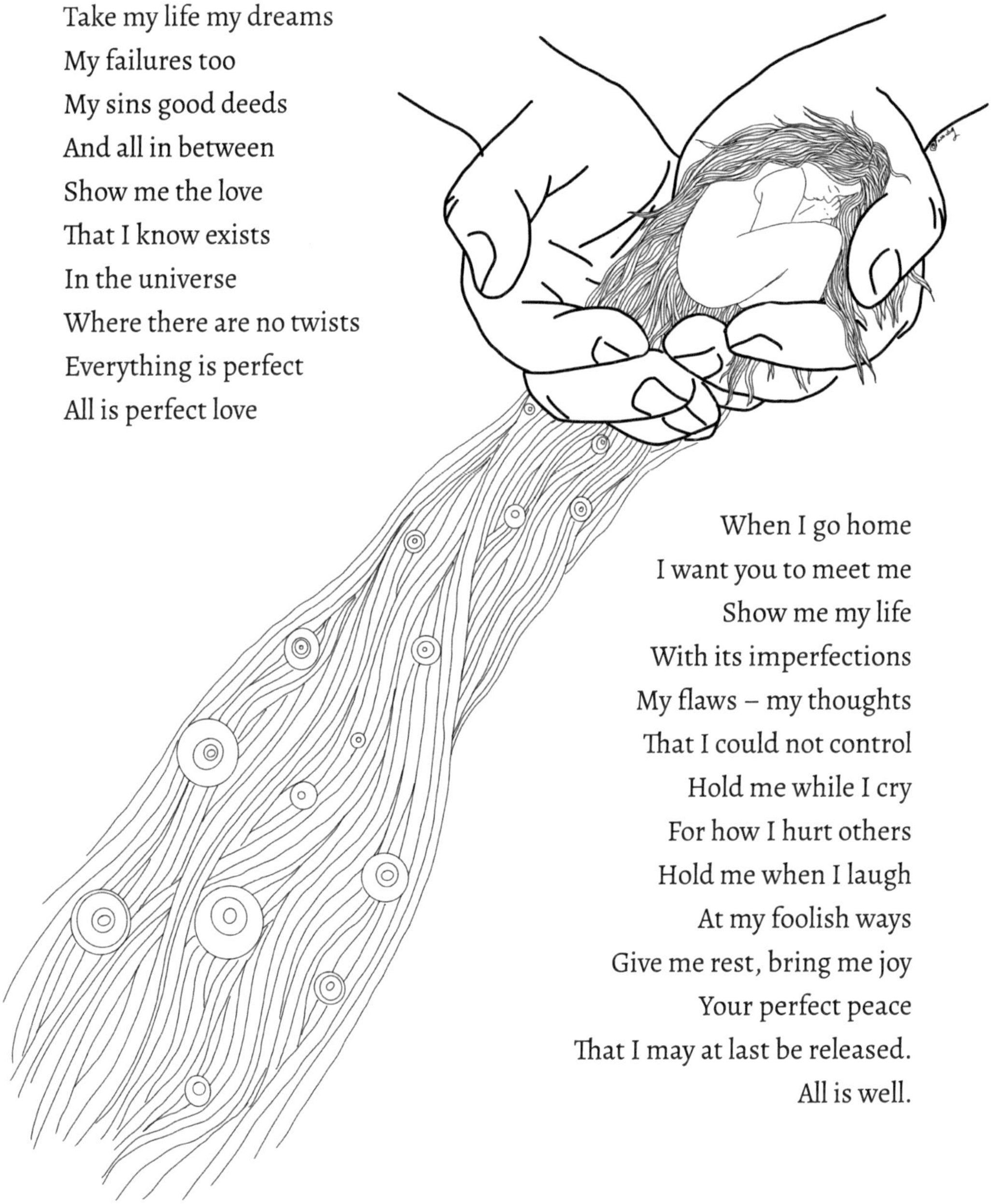

When I go home
I want you to meet me
Show me my life
With its imperfections
My flaws – my thoughts
That I could not control
Hold me while I cry
For how I hurt others
Hold me when I laugh
At my foolish ways
Give me rest, bring me joy
Your perfect peace
That I may at last be released.
All is well.